ᐅᐱᐅᖅᑕᖅᑑᔪᑦ ᐃᒪᕐᒥᐅᑕᖏᓐᓂᒃ ᐃᓕᓴᕐᓂᐊᕐᓗᑎᑦ!

UUMAJUT

LEARN ABOUT ARCTIC WILDLIFE!

INHABIT MEDIA
IQALUIT • TORONTO

2

ᐅᑭᐅᖅᑕᖅᑑᑉ ᐆᒪᔪᖏᓐᓂᒃ ᐃᓕᑦᑎᓗᓯ!

UUMAJUT

LEARN ABOUT ARCTIC WILDLIFE!

ᐋᖅᑭᒋᐊᓇᔫᒃ | Edited by

ᓃᓪ ᑯᕆᔅᑕᕗᕐ | Neil Christopher

ᓗᐃᔅ ᕝᓚᕼᐅᕐᑎ | Louise Flaherty

ᑎᑎᕋᖅᑐᕕᓃᑦ | Written by

ᓴᐃᒪᓐ ᐊᕙ | Simon Awa

ᓯᒡᓗᒃ ᐊᕐᑭᐊᒍᖅ | Seeglook Akeeagok

ᐋᓇ ᓯᒡᓗᕐ | Anna Ziegler

ᔅᑎᐊᕙᓂ ᒪᒃᑖᓄᓪᓪ | Stephanie McDonald

ᐃᓄᒃᑎᑑᓕᖅᑎᑕᖕᒋᑦ | Translated by

ᓚᐊ ᐅᑕᒃ | Leah Otak

ᑎᑎᖅᑐᒐᖅᑕᖕᒋᑦ | Illustrated by

ᕉᒥ ᑲᐃᕋᓐ | Romi Caron

2

Published by Inhabit Media Inc.
www.inhabitmedia.com

Toronto Office -191 Eglinton Avenue East, Suite 310, Toronto, Ontario, M4P 1K1
Iqaluit Office - P.O. Box 11125, Iqaluit, Nunavut, X0A 1H0

Design and layout copyright © 2018 by Inhabit Media Inc.
Text copyright © 2018 by Inhabit Media Inc.
Illustrations copyright © 2018 by Romi Caron

Printed and bound in Canada

10 9 8 7 6 5 4 3 2

This book has been published with support from the Qikiqtani Inuit Association, Canada Council for the Arts, Nunavut Bilingual Education Society, the Government of Nunavut - Department of Environment, Nunavut Arctic College, the Department of Fisheries and Oceans, Nunavut Wildlife Management Board, and the Rotary Club of Scarborough North.

Library and Archives Canada Cataloguing in Publication

Uumajut : learn about Arctic wildlife / edited by Neil Christopher, Louise Flaherty ; written by Simon Awa ... [et al.] ; translated by Leah Otak ; illustrated by Romi Caron = Ukiuqtaqtuup uumajunginnik ilittilusi! / aaqkigiarijuuk Niil Kuristavur, Luis Vlahurti ; titiraqtuviniit Saiman Ava ... [et al.] ; inuktituuliqtitangit Lia Utak ; titiqtugaqtangit Ruumi Kairan.

Text in English and Inuktitut (in syllabic characters). Title in Inuktitut romanized.
ISBN 978-1-926569-22-2

1. Animals--Arctic regions--Juvenile literature. 2. Inuit--Nunavut--Juvenile literature. I. Christopher, Neil, 1972- II. Flaherty, Louise III. Awa, Simon IV. Otak, Leah V. Caron, Romi VI. Title: Ukiuqtaqtuup uumajunginnik ilittilusi!.

QL105.U94 2011 j591.70911'3 C2011-900514-X

ᖃᐅᔨᒪᑦᑕ ᐃᓄᐃᑦ ᑲᑐᔾᔨᖃᑎᒌᖏᑦ
Qikiqtani Inuit Association

ᓄᓇᕗᑦ ᓯᓚᑦᑐᖅᓴᕐᕕᒃ
Nunavut Arctic College

Nunavut Wildlife Management Board

IPY·API
International Polar Year
Année polaire internationale
2007·2008 ᓄᓇᕐᔪᐊᑦ ᐅᑭᐅᖅᑕᑐᖓᑦ ᐅᐱᐅᖑᓂ

Canada Council   Conseil des Arts
for the Arts   du Canada

Fisheries and Oceans   Pêches et Océans
Canada   Canada

ᖁᔭᓐᓇᒦᕈᒪᔭᕗᑦ ᐅᖃᓕᒫᒐᖅᒥ ᑖᒃᓯᒥᙵ ᐱᖖᒍᖅᑎᑦᑎᖅᑕᐅᔪᓐᓇᓚᐅᖅᒪᑕ ᓴᓃᓇ ᑖᑦᓯᐊᑦ,
ᐊᓃᓴ ᓲᓄ, ᓕᕖᓇ ᓄᔭᓕᐊ, ᓕᓐᑕ ᒥᐅᑦᑕᓐ-ᖃᔮᖅ.

We thank Sharina Dodsworth, Tyler Ross, Anisa Suno, Leeveena Nuyalia, and Linda Milton-Kyak for their contributions.

ᐃᓄᑦᑐᖕᕆᑦ | Contents

ᑐᕝᖃᑎᑕᖅ |Dedication 2

ᑕᑯᐣᑎᑎᕆᐊᖕᒪᑦᓯᖕᓂᖅ |Introduction 4

ᓂᑎᓇᐅᐸᑦ ᐅᒪᔪᖕᕆᑦ | Animals of the Tundra 7

ᓯᐠᓯᐠ | Siksik 9

ᐅᒥᖕᒪᐠ | Muskox 11

ᑎᓇᐊᖅ | Ermine 13

ᐊᒪᕈᖅ | Wolf 15

ᑕᕆᐅᑉ ᓯᑰᓪᓗ ᐆᒪᔪᖏᑦ | Animals of the Sea and Ice 17
ᒥᑎᖅ | Eider Duck 19
ᓇᑦᑎᖅ | Ringed Seal 21
ᖃᐃᕈᓕᒃ | Harp Seal 23
ᐊᐃᕙᖅ | Walrus 25
ᕿᓚᓗᒐᖅ (ᐊᓪᓚᖑᐊᖅ) | Narwhal 27
ᓇᓄᖅ | Polar Bear 29

ᑐᓂᓯᔪᑦ | Contributors 30

ᑐᕌᖅᑎᑕᖅ | Dedication

ᓯᓪᓗᒃ ᐊᕿᐊᑯᖅ | Seeglook Akeeagok

1955-2010

ᓯᓪᓗᒃ ᐊᕿᐊᑯᖅ ᐃᖅᑲᓇᐃᔩᖅᑲᓚᐅᖅᑐᖅ ᓄᓇᕗᑦ ᒐᕙᒪᒃᑯᑦ ᐊᕙᑎᓕᕆᔨᒃᑯᖓᓐᓄᑦ ᕿᑭᖅᑖᓗᖕᒥ ᐊᐅᓚᑦᑎᔨᐅᓪᓗᓂ. ᐃᖅᑲᓇᐃᔭᓚᐅᖅᑐᖅ ᐆᒪᔪᓕᕆᔨᒃᑯᑦ 30 (ᐊᕙᑎᓪᓗ ᖁᓕᓪᓗ) ᐊᕐᕌᒍᑦ ᐅᖓᑖᓄᑦ, ᐆᒪᔪᑦ ᐊᑐᕐᓂᕐᓗᒃᑕᐅᑦᑕᐃᓕᒪᓂᖏᓐᓂᒃ ᐃᖃᓗᓕᕆᓂᕐᒥᓪᓗ. ᓯᓪᓗᒃ ᐃᓅᓚᐅᖅᓯᒪᔪᖅ ᑕᓯᐅᔭᒥ ᐃᓪᓗᓕᐅᑉ ᖃᓂᒋᔮᓂ ᕿᑭᖅᑖᓗᖕᒥ. ᐱᖓᓱᓂᒃ ᐊᕐᕌᒍᖃᓕᖅᓱᓂ ᐊᐅᓱᐃᑦᑐᒧᑦ ᓅᓚᐅᖅᓯᒪᔪᑦ ᑕᐃᑲᓂᕐᒥᐅᑕᐅᓪᓗᓂᓗ 1975 ᒧᑦ ᑎᑭᕐᓱᒍ. ᑖᔅᓱᒪ ᐃᓚᖏᑦ ᓅᑕᐅᓂᑰᓚᐅᕆᕗᑦ ᐊᐅᓱᐃᑦᑐᒧᑦ. ᓯᓪᓗᒃ ᒥᑦᑎᒪᑕᓕᖕᒥᓗ ᖃᐅᓱᐃᑦᑐᒥᓗ ᓄᓇᖃᓚᐅᕆᕗᖅ ᐃᖃᓗᖕᓄᑦ ᓅᓚᐅᕐᓂᖓᑕ ᓯᕗᕐᖓᓂ ᐃᓚᓂ ᐃᓚᒋᓪᓗᓂᒋᑦ.

ᓯᓪᓗᒃ ᐱᕈᖅᓴᓪᓗᓂ ᐊᖑᓇᓱᒃᐸᓚᐅᖅᑐᖅ ᐊᒻᒪᓗ ᐊᖑᓇᓱᖕᓂᖅ ᖁᕕᐊᒋᓪᓗᓂᐅᒃ ᓱᓕ ᒪᒃᑯᕕᒡᔪᐊᖅᓱᓂ ᐊᖑᓇᓱᒋᐅᖅᓯᒪᒐᒥ. ᐅᒃᐱᕆᔭᖅᑲᓚᐅᖅᑐᖅ ᒪᒃᑯᒃᑐᑦ ᖃᐅᔨᒪᑦᑎᐊᖁᓪᓗᒋᑦ ᑲᒪᑦᑎᐊᖁᓪᓗᒋᓪᓗ ᐆᒪᔪᓂᓪᓗ ᐊᕙᑎᑦᑎᓐᓂᓪᓗ ᐊᒻᒪ ᐃᓄᐃᑦ ᐃᓕᖅᑯᓯᖓᑦᑎᒍᑦ ᑕᒪᒃᑯᐊ ᖃᐅᔨᔭᐅᑎᕐᓱᓂᒋᑦ ᒪᒃᑯᒃᑐᓄᑦ.

Seeglook Akeeagok was the regional manager of wildlife for Qikiqtaaluk (Baffin Region) for the Government of Nunavut Department of Environment. He worked in wildlife conservation for over 30 years, both as a conservation officer and a fisheries officer. Seeglook was born at Murray Maxwell Bay on Baffin Island. At the age of three, he moved to Grise Fiord and lived there until 1975. His family was one of many that were relocated to Grise Fiord from Northern Baffin Island. Seeglook also lived in Pond Inlet and Resolute Bay before coming to Iqaluit with his family.

Seeglook grew up hunting and was an avid hunter from a very young age. He believed in educating youth about wildlife and environmental stewardship and actively promoted the transfer of traditional Inuit knowledge of wildlife to youth. He was involved in a number of education programs and projects, and he contributed a great deal of his

ᐃᑐᐅᖅᑕᑕᐅᕐᒪᑕ ᐊᒥᓱᓄᑦ ᐃᓕᓴᓂᐊᕈᑎᓄᑦ
ᐱᑕᓕᐊᔪᒃᔪᓄᑦᓗ, ᐃᑲᔫᒥᓂᖅᑕᑕᐅᖅᑐᖅ
ᖃᐅᔨᒪᓂᕐᓄᑦ ᓱᓚᑐᓂᕐᓄᑦᓗ ᑖᔅᓱᒻᖕ ᐅᖃᑕᐅᖕᕐᒍᑦ
ᐊᑎᖅᖅᑐᒃᑦ ᐆᒪᔪᑦ, ᐱᖑᔪᑦᓯᒍᑦ.

ᐆᒪᔪᑦ, ᐱᖑᔪᑎᖅ ᑐᒢᖅᑎᑕᕐᑦ ᓯᒡᓗᒃ
ᐊᖅᐊᒍᕐᒍᑦ, ᐃᖅᑲᐅᒪᕐᔮᓯᑎᐊᕞᐅᓄᐊᕐᒪᑦ
ᐱᑕᓂᐊᓕᓂᖏᑦ ᓯᐴᓚᑎᖕᓂ ᓯᕐ ᐆᒪᕐᓂᐊᕐᓂᕐᒍᑦ
ᖃᐅᔨᒪᔪᐸᔪᑎᐊᓕᖕᓂᖅ ᐊᒻᓗ ᓄᓇᕘᒥ ᐊᔾᔨᐅᖕᒥᖕᓂᖕ
ᐆᒪᔪᑦ ᐱᓕᖑᑎᑦ.

knowledge and wisdom toward the creation of this book, *Uumajut, Volume Two.*

Uumajut, Volume Two is dedicated to Seeglook Akeeagok, whose legacy will inspire many more wildlife education projects that will help people understand and appreciate the unique wildlife of Nunavut.

ᓯᒡᓗᒃᑲᒃ ᐃᕐᖑᑕᕐᓚᑦᖕ.
Seeglook and his grandson.

ᑕᑯᓐᑎᑎᕐᐊᖕᒦᕐᓂᖅ | Introduction

Cᒫᓂ ᓄᓇ�ᒥ ᑕᒫᑦᑕ ᓄᓇ ᐃᒻᕐᓗ ᐊᑐᖅᐸ�᠍ᑲᑕᖅᐳᑦ ᐊ᠍ᒪᓪᒪᑕᐅᖅ ᐅᒪᔪᑦ ᑕᒫᓂᖅᑎᑎᕐᓚᔪ᠍ᑎ ᐊᔾᐱ᠍ᖕᑎᕆᔪᔾᖃᖅᔪᑦ ᐊᔾᐊᖃ᠍ᖕᑎᔪᒡᓗ ᓄᓇᕐᖁᒦ ᐃᓕᖅᑯᓯᕐᖕᓂᖕᓂᖕᑦ ᐃᓕᖅᑯᓯᖅᑲᓐᖕᑐᑎᖕᑦ. ᐃᓕᖕᕐᑦ ᐃᑰᔪᓯᒪᑎᖕᑦ ᑕᒫᓂ ᐅᑭᐅᖅᑕᖅᑐᒡᒥᐅᑕᐅᖃᖅᔪᑦ ᐃᒪᖕᓗᓂ, ᐃᓕᖕᕐᑦᑕᐅᖅ ᑕᒪᐅᖕᓚᐅᖃᖕᑐᖕᑦ ᐅᖕᓗᔭᖕᑐᐊᓗᖕᒡᓚᑦ ᓂᖅᑲᓂᖅᔾᐅᖅᖕᑐᖕᑦ. ᑕᒡᖁᐊ ᐅᒪᔮᑦ ᑕᐅᑐᖕᕐᐸᖕᑲᖕᒡᖁᑦ ᐃᓂᕆᖃᖕᖕᑦᖕᕐᓗ ᐃᓕᖕᕐᕐᑕᐊᓚᖕᑐᐅᖅ ᔾᓚᖕᕐᐊᖕᓗᓂᖅ ᑐᑭᓯᐊᖕᓇᖕᓯᖕᓕᖕᖃᖕᑕᖕᖅᐸᖕᑦ.

ᐅᒪᔾᖁᑦ ᐃᓕᖕᕐᕐᑕᐊᓚᖕᕐᐅᕐ ᐃᑰᔾᓚᖕᓚᖕᓂ ᖅᑯᐊᐊᕆᖕᒡᑐᔾᖁ. ᓄᑲᖕᕐᐱᐊᖕᔾᑐᕐᖕᓗ ᐃᓕᖕᕐᓂ ᐃᓕᐅᖕᕐᕐᑕᐅᖕᖕᕐ᠍ᖕᓗ ᐊᔾᖁᓇᖕᕐᑐᓂ ᑭᓯᐅᖕᕐᖕᓂᖕᖃᖕᑦᖕᕐᐊᓇᖕᓂᖕᖅᐸᖕᑦ ᑕᐅᑐᖕᕐᐸᖕᑲᖕᒡᖁᑦᖃᑲᖕᑦ. ᑲᒪᔾᖃᖕᕐ᠍ᐊᐅᖕᕐᕐᒃᖕᓗ ᖁᖃᖕᓯ ᐅᒪᔾᖁᓇᖕᕐᐸᖕᓂᖕᖕᕐᑦ ᑕᒫᓂ ᓂᖕᕐᓚᖕᕐᑐᑕᓚᖕᖁᕐᒥ. ᑐᖕᓯᓂᕐᐊᐅᖕᕐᕐᐸᖕᓗᖕᕐ ᐊᖕᖁᐊᐃᑦ, ᐊᔾᖁᓇᖕᕐᖕᑎᖕᓗ, ᐃᓕᕆᖕᕐᔾᑐᖕᕐᓗ ᐅᐊᖕᕐᓂᖕᕐ ᐃᓚᖕᑎᖕᑎᖕᑎᖕᖁᕐᒪᖕᕐ ᐊᔾᐱ᠍ᖕᑎᖕᑐᑎᖕᑐᒡ ᐃᓄᐃᑦ ᐅᒪᓇᖕᔾᖁᖕᕐᓂᖕᕐ ᑭᓯᐊᓂ ᐊᔾᖁᓇᖕᔾᖕᑐᖕᑎᖕ. ᖅᑲᐅᔾᖃᖕᓚᖕᕐᐊᖕᓂᖕᕐ ᐅᒪᔾᖁᖕᕐ ᐊᔾᐱ᠍ᖕᑎᖕᑎᖕᕐᐊᖕᔾᑯᓚᖕᕐᔾᖕ. ᒫᖕᑕ ᐅᒪᔾᖁᖕᕐ ᐊᑐᖕᕐᐊᖕᖕᑕᐃᑎᓚᖕᖁᖕᕐᕐ ᐃᖃᖕᓇᐃᖕᕐᖃᖕᓗᖕᓚᐃ

ᓄᓇᕗᒻᒥᐅᖅᑎᓐᓂᓂᒃ ᐱᓕᕆᖃᑎᖃᑦᑎᖅᐳᖓ
ᖃᓄᐃᓕᓂᖏᓕᖏᑕ ᐊᒻᓚ ᓄᔾᐸᑕᐊᖅᑕᕐᑎᓐᐹᔪᑎᐅᖅᑕᓐᓂᒃ ᓄᓇᕗᒥ ᑕᒫᓂᓴᓲ.
ᑕᐧᐁᓂ ᐅᖃᓕᒫᓂᒐᒥ, ᐅᒪᒃᑦ ᑭᔾᑎᓇᒐᒥ,
ᖃᐅᔨᒃᑲᓂᓂᓴᐊᖅᐳᑎ ᐅᒪᒃᑦ ᑕᒫᓄᐸᐸᑎᐅᖕᒋᑏᑕ ᐱᑕᖃᓴᖅᐸᓴᓇᐊᓂᖕᓂ ᓄᓇᕗᒥ. ᑕᐱᒪᓕᑦ ᖄᑯᐊᕋᓂᐊᖅᐸᑦ ᖃᐅᔨᕐᖃᓵᕋᐊᒍᔾᑎᑕᐃᓴᒃᖅᑕᑦᕙᖅᑯᑏ ᐱᓕᕆᒪᔅᕆᔭᐅᑎ ᐃᓕᑎᑦᒐ ᖃᐅᔨᑏᓇᓴᓇᐊᓴᐸᑐᑏᑕᐊ ᐱᑦᐊᖅᑕᓇᓂᖅᑐᑕ ᓄᓇᕗᒥ.

ᑎᐅ ᐃᑯᒻᒪᖅ

Theo Ikummaq

as a conservation officer, I work with other Nunavummiut to help monitor and preserve wildlife so that they may continue to thrive in Nunavut.

In this book, the second in the Uumajut series, you will learn about an interesting collection of wildlife species found throughout Nunavut. Enjoy learning more about these amazing animals, and be sure to share this book with your friends and family. I hope that the information and illustrations contained within this book will inspire you and help you gain a new appreciation for Nunavut's treasured wildlife.

ᓇᑎᒐᐅᑉ ᑐᒪᔪᖏᑦ
Animals of the Tundra

ᓯᑲᓯᒃ | Siksik

ᓯᒃᒃᔾᑦᑦᐅᓱ ᖃᐃᓪᒍᖓᒃᐱᑎᒪ ᐊᑎᖅᑲᑯ "Arctic ground squirrel." ᓯᒃᔾᑦ ᓄᓇᐃᐅᓂᖅᓕᒐ ᓄᓇᕐᒥ ᐱᑕᖅᑲᔾᐅᖕᑕ ᑭᔾᐊᓂ ᖅᑭᖅᑕᓂᔾᐅᔪᖆᖕᑕᑐᑦ. ᐃᓪᒃ ᑲᑎᖕᖕᔾᑦ ᐊᒻᒪ ᓴᖃᖅᑕᑎᔾᔾᔾᑦᑐᖕᑕ. ᑎᔾᑕᐅᔾᑦ ᐃᒎᐊᔪᑦ ᐊᒌᓂᖕ ᐊᖕᒍᖅᔾᖅᑕᐅᖅᑐᖕᑐᖕ ᐊᒻᒪ ᐊᖕᑲᔾᒪᔭᓂᖕ ᐱᓲᖕᖃᑕᐅᖅᖕᑐᖕ. ᐅᑭᐅᒃᑕᑦ ᓯᖕᓇᓄᔾᒍᒪᐸᒃ ᑖᖅᑭᓄᑦ 7 ᓄᑦ ᓯᓂᔾᑦ. ᓯᓂᖕᓄᐊᖅᑐᖕ ᐃᒎᔾᑦ ᐊᖃᒍᖅᒃᒍᖕᑐᖕ ᐊᖅᓴᑎᔾᑦ ᐸᒥᐅᖕᓄᑦ ᓂᐊᖅᑎᖕ ᑎᑎᑎᓪᔾ ᐅᑕᖅᔭᒪᔾᒍᖕ. ᐊᐅᔾᖅᑯᑦ ᓯᒃᔾᑦ ᓂᕆᔾᔾᔾᐅᔾᖕᑐᖕ ᐅᖅᐅᔭᓂᖕ, ᓄᕿᓴᓂᖕ, ᓇᕝᑯᓂᖕ, ᐊᒪᓂᖕ, ᐸᐅᕐᖕᓯᓂᖕᔾ. ᐃᒡᖕᓂᖕᑲᑦᑦ ᒪᖕᖕᑎᔾᑦ ᖅᑯᕝᓄᐊᓂᖕᔾ. ᓯᒃᔾᑦ ᐱᔾᖕᓂᖕᖃᖕᑕᖕᑲᖕᑦᑕᑐᖕ ᑎᔾᖕᓂᖕᖕᖕᑎᖕᑲᑦᑕᕐᔾᖕᓚᑦ, ᓄᓇᔾᑦ ᐊᕐᑕᑐᖕ ᖕᑲᑦᔾᑦ ᐃᔾᔾᔾᒪᔾᑦᑐᖕ ᐊᖙᓇᔾᔾᓂᖕ ᖃᒃᓇᖃᓚ. ᖃᒃᖃ ᐊᒡᖕᑕᖕᖃᔾᑦᑦ ᐳᐃᔾᔾᔾᔾᔾᒍᖕᑦᑕᑦ. ᖃᒡᖕᖃᓂᖕ ᐃᑲᖅᔾᔾᔾᒍᖕᑦᑕᑦ.

"Siksik" is another name for the Arctic ground squirrel. Siksiks live on the mainland of Nunavut, but not on the islands. They live in family groups and work together. They make underground homes with many rooms and tunnels. They hibernate in their homes for about seven months of the year. To hibernate, a siksik rolls up into a ball and uses its tail to cover its head and shoulders. In the summer, siksiks eat leaves, flowers, stems, roots, and berries. Sometimes they also eat eggs and small birds. When siksiks are outside of their safe homes, they travel low to the ground to hide from predators. These little burrowers can also swim. They often cross small streams in their travels.

ᐅᒥᖕᒪᒃ | Muskox

ᐅᒥᖕᒪᐃᑦ ᑕᒫᓂ ᓄᓇᑦᑎᓐᓂᒥᐅᑕᐅᓚᖅᐳᑦ 90,000 ᓂᒃ ᐊᕐᕌᒍᓂᒃ. ᑖᒃᑯᐊ ᖃᐅᔨᑲᐅᑎᒋᔭᒃᓴᐅᕗᑦ ᑭᓲᖕᒪᖕᒌᑕ ᓇᒡᔪᖕᒋᑦ ᓂᐅᖕᒐᖕᒪᑕ ᒥᖅᑯᖕᒋᓪᓗ ᑐᕐᕿᓪᓗᑎᒃ. ᒥᖅᑯᖕᒋᑦ ᓯᓚᓪᓛᑦ ᑕᑭᔫᑕᐅᓪᓗᑎᒃ ᕿᕐᓂᕐᓂᖅᓴᐅᓪᓗᑎᒡᓗ ᐊᒻᒪ ᓱᕐᒃᓴᕐᐃᙱᑐᑦ ᓯᓚᒥ ᐊᒻᒪᓗ ᐃᓗᓪᓖᑦ ᒥᖅᑯᖕᒋᑦ ᓇᐃᑦᑑᑎᐅᓪᓗᑎᒃ ᐊᒃᓯᐊᓗᒃ ᐅᖅᑰᔦᑦ. ᐅᒥᖕᒪᐃᑦ ᓂᐅᖕᒋᑦ ᓇᐃᑦᑐᑯᓗᐃᑦ ᑭᓯᐊᓂ ᓴᙱᔦᒪᓇᐊᓗᐃᑦ. ᐃᓯᒐᖕᒋᑕ ᑯᑭᖕᒋᑦ ᐃᐱᒃᑐᐊᓗᐃᑦ ᐱᓚᓇᑎᓪᓗᒋᑦ ᐅᔭᖅᑲᓂᒃ, ᐊᐳᒻᒥᒃ ᑎᓯᔦᒥᒃ ᐅᕝᕘᓐᓃᑦ ᓯᑯᒥᒃ ᐱᓚᓇᔭᓇᐊᖅᑲᕙᖕᒐᒥᒃ. ᓱᒃᑲᐃᑦᑐᑰᓪᓗᑎᒃ ᐃᖕᒋᕐᕋᓲᑦ ᑭᓯᐊᓂ ᐸᖕᒐᓕᒍᓐᓇᕐᒥᔦᑦ ᐊᒻᒪ ᒪᔦᕈᓐᓇᖅᓗᑎᒃ. ᑲᑉᐱᐊᓯᓚᕚᖕᒐᒥᒃ, ᑲᑎᓲᑦ ᐃᓐᓇᐃᑦ ᓯᓚᓪᓚᐅᓪᓗᑎᒃ ᐊᖕᒪᓗᖅᓯᓪᓗᑎᒃ ᐱᐊᕋᖕᒋᑦ ᐃᓗᓪᓚᐅᓪᓗᑎᒃ ᑖᒃᑯᐊ ᐃᓐᓇᐃᑦ ᐅᖕᒐᒧᑦ ᓵᙵᓪᓗᑎᒃ, ᐱᐊᕋᒥᖕᓂᒃ ᑕᐃᒪᓐᓇ ᐅᖖᒪᓰᑦ ᓇᒡᔪᖕᒥᖕᓄᑦᑐ ᐊᖏᓂᕐᒥᖕᓄᑦᑐ. ᐅᒥᖕᒪᐃᑦ ᓄᓇᓂᒃ ᓂᕿᓲᑦ, ᒪᑯᓂᖕᒐ ᐅᖃᐅᔭᓂᒃ, ᐃᕙᖕᓂᒃ ᐊᒻᒪ ᐱᕈᖅᓯᐊᒃᓴᓂᒃ. ᐅᒥᖕᒪᐃᑦ ᐊᖑᓇᓱᒃᑕᐅᕙᒃᑐᑦ ᓂᕿᖕᒋᓐᓄᑦ ᐊᒻᒪ ᐊᒥᓐᓄᑦ. ᒥᖅᑯᐃᔭᕌᖕᒐᑕ ᐊᐅᔭᒃᑯᑦ ᒥᖅᑯᖕᒋᑕ ᐊᕝᕗᖅᑕᐅᕙᒃᑐᑦ. ᒥᖅᑯᖕᒐᑕ ᐃᓪᓗᓪᓚᖕᒐ ᑕᐃᔭᐅᕙᒃᑐᑦ ᑭᕕᐅᓂᒃ ᐅᖅᑰᓪᓗᑎᒃ ᓂᕈᒥᒃᓗᑎᒡᓗ.

Muskoxen have lived in the Arctic for over 90,000 years. They are easy to recognize by their curved horns and shaggy coats. Their coats have two layers of hair. The dark, outer coat hair is long and coarse to protect against harsh winds. The undercoat hair is short, soft, and wooly to keep the muskox warm through cold winters. Muskoxen are short but very strong. Their hooves have sharp edges to help them grip rocks, hard snow, and ice. Muskoxen usually move slowly, but they can run and climb well when necessary. When a herd of muskoxen is threatened, the animals gather together with the adults on the outside. The young stay in the middle and the adults face outward, using their size and horns to protect the herd. Muskoxen eat tundra plants, such as willows, grasses, and seeds. Muskoxen are hunted for meat and for their coat. Their undercoat hair is also gathered from the land as it is shed. The undercoat hairs are known as *qiviut* and are valued for their softness and warmth.

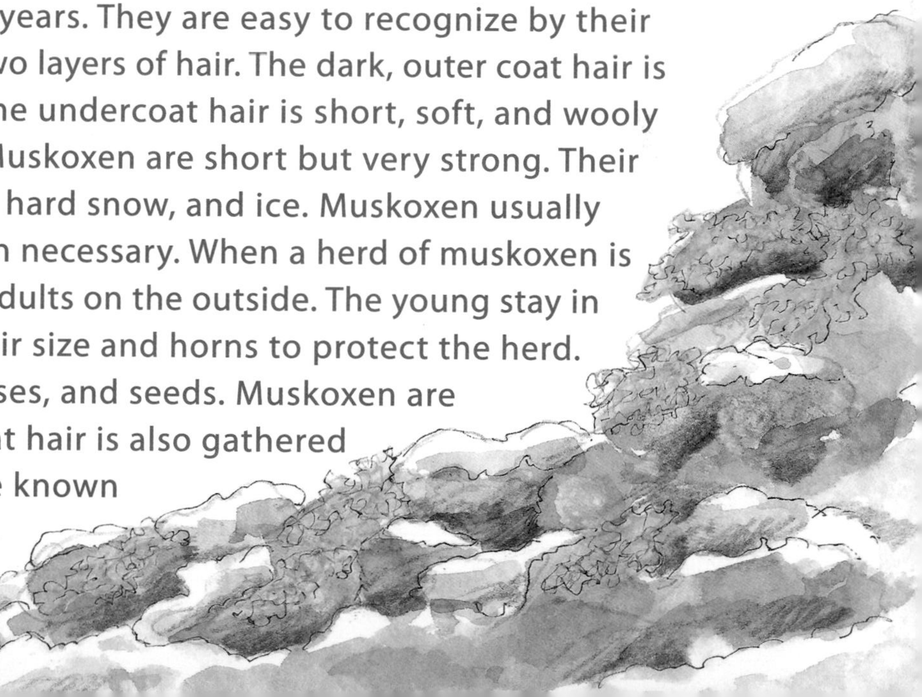

ᑎᓕᐊᖅ | Ermine

ᑕᒻᒃᑯᐊ ᑎᓕᐊᑦ ᐊᖓᓇᕐᒃᐸᒃᑑᑦ ᑖᒻᓂ ᓄᓇᒥ. ᑎᓕᐊᑦ ᑎᒥᖏᑦ ᑕᑭᓗᑏᑦ ᑐᐊᕐᑑᑎᑦ, ᓂᐅᖕᒥᑦ ᓇᐃᑦᑐᑯᔫᓗᑎᑦ. ᑖᓚᐅᒻᒪᑦ ᑎᒻᖕᓕᑦ ᑖᓚᐅᓕᓇᖕᒐ ᐃᒃᔪᑎᖅᖃᑐᖅ ᔅᖃᓂᖕᓗᓄᑦ ᐊᒻᒪ ᒥᑦᑐᑯᓄᖃᑎᒍᑦ ᐱᔪᒪᔭᒻᓂᒃ ᐱᔪᒪᔨᒍᑕᑦ. ᓄᓇᕗᒻᒥ ᑎᓕᐊᑦ ᐊᖓᓇᔾᔨᑦ ᐊᕐᖕᓕᓂᒃ ᖅᑯᕐᓄᐊᓂᒃ, ᐅᑲᓕᕐᓂᒃ, ᔅᒃᓯᓂᓗ. ᑎᓕᐊᑦ ᑲᔾᔨᔫᑦ ᓅᖕᑎᑦ ᖅᑲᐅᑦᓗᖅᑐᑎᑦ. ᐅᑭᐊᖅᖃᑯᑦ ᖅᑲᐅᑦᓗᖅᒃᐸᑦᖅ ᑭᒃᐊᓂ ᐸᒼᐳᖕᓕᑦ ᓄᕼᐊ ᖅᕐᓇᓐᓇᖅᑐᓂ. ᑎᓕᐊᑦ ᐃᖕᓂᔾᔫᑦ ᐊᖅᖓᓴᓐᓂᑦ ᖅᑕᓄᑦ ᐅᓇᖅᖃᖅᑐᓂᒃ.ᑎᓕᐊᑦ ᐃᖒᖕᓯᖕᒪᒻᑉᒃ, ᑕᐅᑐᖖᒃᑎᔾᑦ ᑐᖕᓇᑎᖕᓗ. ᐊᔾᒑᖖᒃᖅᐸᖕᑐᑎᒃ ᐃᖒᖕᒥᖕᔾᖕᑎᒐᖕᒪᒻᑉᒃ.

The ermine (also known as the weasel) is a daring little hunter that lives on the tundra. Ermine have long, thin bodies with short legs. This body shape helps them move quickly and squeeze into small burrows to catch their prey. In Nunavut, ermine hunt for lemmings, small birds, Arctic hares, and siksiks. In the summer, the ermine is brown with a white belly. In the fall, the ermine turns all white, except for the tip of its tail, which remains black. Ermine mothers have litters of six to ten babies. When ermine are born, their eyes and ears are shut. They open after a few weeks.

ᐊᒪᕈᖅ | Wolf

ᐊᒪᕐᑯᑦ ᕿᒧᒃᓯᐅᑎᑎᑐᑦ ᕿᒻᒥᑎᑐᑦ ᑕᐃᒪᐃᑉᐳᑦ, ᓂᐅᖏᑦ ᑕᑭᓂᖅᓴᐅᑦᑐᑎᒃ ᐃᓯᒐᖏᑦᑐ ᐊᖏᓂᖅᓴᐅᑦᑐᑎᒃ. ᒥᕐᑯᖏᑦ ᐅᖅᑰᔭᐊᓘᕗᑦ ᐅᑭᐅᖅᑕᖅᑐᒥ ᐅᖅᑰᔮᓐᓇᖅᑐᑎᒃ. ᐊᒪᕐᑯᑦ ᐊᒥᓲᑦᑐᑎᒃ ᑲᑎᙵᐸᒃᐳᑦ ᐊᑕᐅᑦᓯᒥ. ᑲᑐᔾᔨᑦᑐᑎᒃ ᐊᖑᓇᓱᓲᖑᕗᑦ ᓂᕿᑎᓂᒃ ᐊᖏᖅᑭᓴᒥᖕᓂᒃ ᓱᒃᑲᖅᑭᓴᒥᖕᓂᓪᓗ ᒪᑯᓂᖓ ᓲᕐᓗ ᑐᒃᑐᓂᒃ ᐅᒥᖕᒪᖕᓂᓪᓗ. ᒪᓕᒃᐸᒃᐳᑦ ᑐᑦᑐᓂᒃ ᐋᓐᓂᐊᖅᑐᓂᓪᓘᓐᓃᑦ ᓱᒃᑲᐃᓐᓂᖅᓴᓂᓪᓘᓐᓃᑦ ᐱᕙᒃᐳᑦ. ᐊᒪᕐᑯᑦ ᐅᖓᓯᒃᑐᐊᓗᖕᒥᑦ ᓂᕿᒃᓴᖅᓯᐅᖅᐸᒃᑐᑦ ᐱᐊᕋᒥᖕᓂᒃ. ᓂᕿᒥᒃ ᐅᑎᐅᔾᔭᕙᒃᐳᑦ ᖃᓂᕐᒦᓂᑎᑦᑐᕆᑦ ᐋᓯᒪᑦᑐᕆᑦᑑᓐᓃᑦ. ᒥᓇᐊᕐᑲᑦᑕᖅᑕᖏᑦ ᐊᒪᕈᐊᕋᐃᑦ ᐊᓗᒃᓯᑲᑕᓕᕚᖓᑕ ᐃᕿᖏᓐᓂᒃ. ᐊᒪᕈᐃᑦ ᒥᐊᓪᒎᕐᓂᖏᓐᓂᒃ, ᑐᑭᓯᓯᒪᔪᕐᑲᓗᐊᙱᓚᖅ ᓱᖕᒪᑦ ᒥᐊᓪᒎᖅᐸᖕᒪᖕᒫᑕ. ᐃᓄᐃᑦ ᐃᓚᖏᑦ ᑲᖐᓱᒃᐸᒃᐳᑦ ᒥᐊᒡᒎᕋᐅᑎᓱᕆᑦᑎᑦᑐᑎᒃ ᕿᓂᕐᓂᐊᕐᒪᑕ ᐊᓯᐅᖅᑲᔪᓂᒃ ᐊᒪᕈᐊᕋᕐᓂᒃ ᐅᕝᕙᓘᓐᓃᑦ ᐊᖑᓇᓱᐊᕐᓂᐊᕐᒪᑕ. ᐃᓄᐃᑦ ᐃᓚᖏᑦ ᒥᐊᒡᒎᕈᒻᒪᐅᓯᕆᑦᑎᑐᐃᓐᓇᖅᐳᑦ. ᐊᒪᕈᓴᐃᑦ ᓄᐃᓚᓕᐊᕆᔭᐅᕙᒃᐳᑦ ᐸᐊᓗᓕᐊᖑᕙᒃᑐᑎᓪᓗ ᑲᓂᖅᓴᖃᐃᖏᒻᒪᑕ.

Wolves look like sled dogs, but have longer legs and bigger feet. They have very thick fur to keep them warm in the cold Arctic winter. Wolves live in groups called packs. They use teamwork to catch animals that are bigger and faster than they are, such as caribou and muskoxen. They often follow herds, catching the sick or weak caribou. Wolves travel great distances to get food for their pups. They carry the food back in their mouths or stomachs. The food comes up again when the pup licks the corners of the adult's mouth. No one is certain what the purpose of the wolf's distinctive howl is. Some people guess that wolves howl to call each other together to search for lost pups or to hunt. Other people say that maybe wolves just love to howl. Wolf fur is used for trimming parkas and mittens because it does not gather frost.

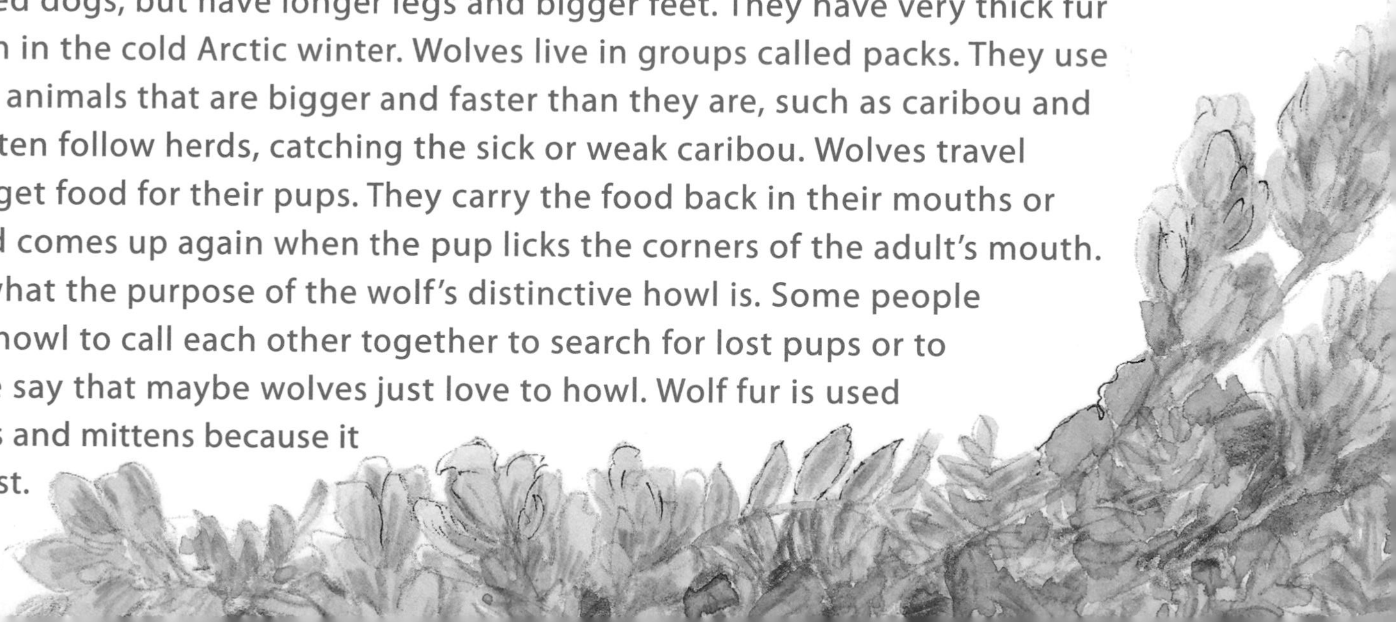

ᑕᕆᐅᑉ ᓯᑰᓪᓗ ᐆᒪᔪᖏᑦ
Animals of the Sea and Ice

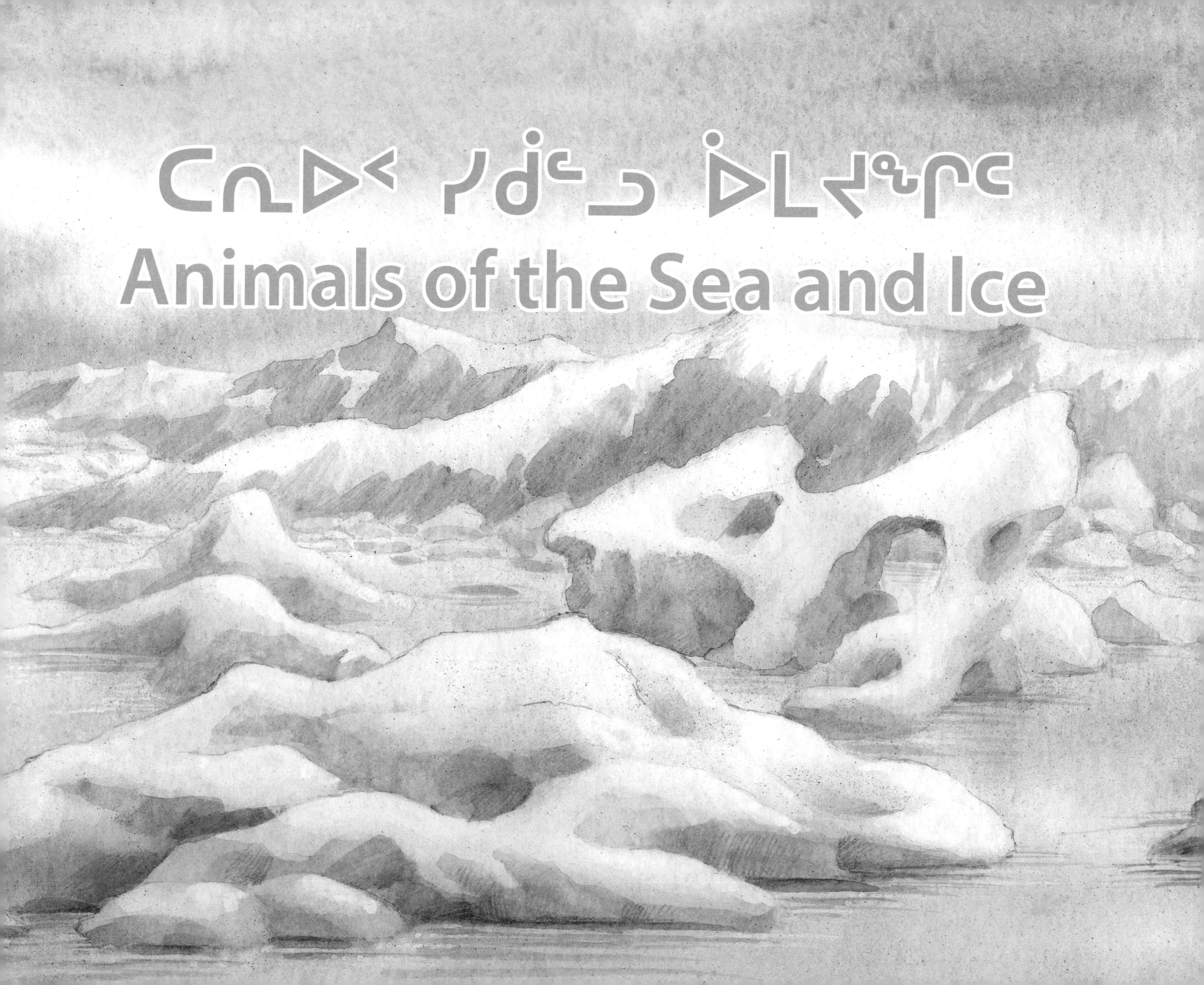

ᒥᑎᖅ | Eider Duck

ᒥᑎᖅᓂ ᐊᐅᐸᓛᕈᐊᑦ ᐊᖏᓛᖑᓪᖅᑦ ᑕᒪᓂ ᓄᓇᑦᑎᓂ, ᐊᒻᒪᑦᑕᐅᖅ ᑖᒃᑯᐊ ᐃᒪᕐᒥᐅᑕᕐᓂ ᑎᖕᒥᐊᖅᖃᑎᒋᓛᕆᓂᑦ ᐃᐆᔪᕐᓯᓂᖅᖃᖁᔪᖅᐅᑦ – ᐊᕐᒡᔪᒍᑦ ᐊᕕᑎᓂᑦ ᐃᐆᔪᕐᓇᕐᒐᑦ! ᐊᖕᒎᑎᑕᐊᑦ ᑕᖅᓴᖕᒥᑦ ᐃᒪᐃᐸᐳᑦ, ᖅᒥᓂᕐᓂᖅᖅᖑᑎᑦ, ᑐᒃᔪᒃᐸᖅᑐᖅᖅᖑᑎᑦ, ᐊᐳᐸᖅᑐᖅᖅᖑᑎᑦ ᐊᒻᒪ ᖅᑲᑦᓄᑐᖅᖅᖑᑎᑦ. ᐸᒧᓕᒥᖅ ᓄᓇᒥ ᐃᕟᑐᑎᑦ ᑕᖅᓴᐳᕐᖑᑎᓛᑦ. ᐱᓇᔪᐊᑉᔪᑦ ᐱᖕᓚᔪᑦ ᑕᐃᓚᖁᓇ ᐃᕟᕐᖅᔪᑦ. ᖅᑭᓚᕐᖅᔪᑦ ᓚᓂᖕᒥᕐᓂᑦ ᐅᒡᔫ ᓚᖅᐸ ᐱᖕᓚᔫᔾᓂᖏᑦ ᐂᔆᖕᓪᑕ ᐃᒋᑎᐊᖅᑐᖅᖑᑎᑦ ᐱᖅᐊᓂ ᓂᓕᖅᖅᐸᓛᑎᑐᑦ ᓚᖕᒥᕐᑦ ᑐᐳᓚᑐᖅᑎᖑᓚᕐᑦ (ᑎᖕᒥᐊᕐᔪᑐᐅᖅᑎᖑᓚᕐᑦ) ᐊᕿᓇᐊᐸᑦ ᓚᖕᒃᑖᓚᑐᖅᖑᑐᑦ ᐃᑲᕐᖅᐸᒃᑐᑦ ᐱᐊᕐᖅᖅᑐᖏᒃ. ᐊᖅᖃᐳᓚᓐᑐᑦ ᓂᓇᖅᐳᑦ ᓚᑯᓂᖕᓚ ᐊᒪᒃᓚᕐᑦ, ᓇᐳᑦᖃᑦ, ᑕᓐᒧᐳᖃᑦ, ᒥᖅᑯᑦᖃᑦ ᐊᒧᓛᖕᓚᓗ. ᐂᔆᕐᖅᔪᑦ ᐃᓄᐃᑎᓐᖅ ᐱᕐᐸᓂ ᐊᕿᐊᐳᐊᓂ ᓯᕐᓯᑎᖅᖅᔪᑦ. ᒥᑎᑦ ᐊᒥᓯᐊᔾᓐᖅᖑᑎᑦ ᖅᖅᓚᑕᕐᖅᔪᑦ ᑲᑎᒪᕐᑦ ᑕᒪᓂ 1000ᓂᖅ ᐅᖕᓚᕐᓂᖅᖅᑐᑦ ᖅᖅᓚᑕᕐᖅᖑᑎᑦ. ᕐᓚ ᓂᑲᓚᕐᖅᑎᕐᓚᒍ ᐸᒃᖅᖃᑕᑕᑎᓐᖅᖑᑎᑦ ᐅᖅᒤᓚᖅᖃᑦᑕᕐᖅᑐᑦ. ᒥᑎᑦ ᕐᑐᓇᒍᕐᑦ ᐊᑐᖅᑕᐅᖅᖅᔪᑦ ᐊᖕᓄᕐᓚᐊᔪᓐᖅᖑᑎᑦ ᐊᒻᒪ ᖅᐱᓚᐊᑎᕐᐸᐊᓐᖅᖑᑎᑦ. ᓚᓂᖕᒥᕐᑦ ᒪᒪᖅᑐᐊᓗᐃᑦ. ᐱᑭᐅᕐᐸᕐᓇᖅᖅᑑᑦ ᓚᓂᖕᒥᕐᓂᖅ ᑕᒪᓂ ᕐᓂ ᖅᑭᑦᖕᓚᓂᑦ ᓄᖕᒨᐊᖏᓂᖅ ᓚᓂᖅᖅᐸᖅᑐᑦ.

The eider duck is the largest duck in the northern hemisphere. It lives longer than any other sea duck—up to twenty years! Male eider ducks have black, green, pink, and white feathers. Females have only brown feathers. This helps them hide in plants and rocks when they sit on their eggs. They sit on their eggs for three weeks. They leave to drink water only every two or three days and they do not eat until the eggs have hatched. Females that have not laid eggs help others raise their ducklings. Eider ducks dive underwater to get mussels, crabs, scallops, sea urchins, and starfish. They swallow them whole and crush them inside their stomachs. Eider ducks fly in huge flocks of more than 1000 ducks. In cold weather, they huddle together in very tight groups to stay warm. Eider duck feathers and skin are used to make clothing and sacks. The eggs are delicious. The best time to gather them is from the middle to the end of June.

ᓇᑦᑎᖅ | Ringed Seal

ᓇᑦᑏᑦ ᐳᐃᔨᓂᑦ ᒥᑭᓐᓂᖅᐹᙳᕗᑦ ᐅᑭᐅᖅᑕᖅᑐᒥ. ᓇᑦᑏᑦ ᐃᓂᐊᙳᕋᒃᑐᑦ ᓄᓇᖅᔭᓂ, ᐊᕐᓇᖕᒋᓐᓄᑦ ᓴᓇᔭᐅᓂᑯᓂᒃ. ᒥᖅᑯᖕᒋᑦ ᖃᐅᓪᓗᖅᖢᑎᒃ ᑭᓯᐊᓂ ᕿᓪᓕᖅᓯᕋᓪᓕᐊᓪᓗᑎᒃ. ᐃᓐᓇᐃᓪᓕ ᓇᑦᑏᑦ ᓯᐊᕐᓇᐅᓪᓗᑎᒃ ᕿᕐᓂᖅᑐᓂᒃ ᑐᓄᐊᒍᑦ ᑕᖅᓴᖅᑲᐅᖅᖢᑎᒃ ᐃᓅᓵᕐᓂᑰᓂᕐᒥᖕᓂᑦ ᐊᒻᒪ ᑕᖅᑮᖕᓄᑦ ᒪᕐᕉᖕᓄᑦ ᐊᕐᓇᒥᖕᓃᑉᐸᒃᑐᑦ ᐊᓯᐃᑖᒃ ᐃᓄᑑᔪᓐᓇᖅᓯᓪᓗᑎᒃ. ᐅᑭᐅᒃᑯᑦ ᓯᑰᑉ ᐊᑖᓃᓯᑦ ᑕᕆᐅᒥ. ᐊᒡᒐᒃᖢᑎᒃ ᓯᑯᒥᒃ ᐊᒡᓗᓕᐅᓯᑦ ᐊᓂᖅᓵᖅᑐᕐᕖᒃᓴᒥᖕᓂᒃ. ᐃᑳᓐᓂᒃᑯᑦ ᐆᑦᑑᓯᑦ ᐊᐳᑎᖅᑲᑦᑎᐊᖅᑎᓪᓗᒍ. ᑭᓯᐊᓂ ᐃᒫᓄᑦ ᐊᖅᑲᑐᐃᓐᓇᕆᐊᖅᑲᐃᓐᓇᖅᐸᒃᑐᑦ ᑭᓯᒥᑦ ᑲᑉᐱᐊᓇᖅᑐᒥᑦ ᐅᐸᒃᑕᐅᒍᑎᒃ. ᐃᓄᖕᓂᑦ ᐊᒃᓱᐊᓗᒃ ᓇᑦᑏᑦ ᐊᑐᕆᔭᐅᓚᐅᖅᐳᑦ ᐃᒻᒪᑲᓪᓚᒃᑲᓐᓂᖅ. ᕿᓯᖕᒋᑦ ᐊᑐᖅᑕᐅᕙᓚᐅᖅᐳᑦ ᓇᑦᑎᕐᑯᓯᐊᖑᓪᓗᑎᒃ ᐸᐊᓗᓕᐊᖑᕋᒃᖢᑎᒡᓗ, ᑲᒥᓪᓕᐊᖑᕋᒃᖢᑎᒡᓗ, ᐊᒻᒪ ᖃᔭᓕᐊᖑᕋᒃᖢᑎᒃ. ᐊᒻᒪᓗ ᐅᖅᓱᖓ ᖁᓪᓕᕐᒧᑦ ᐅᖅᓱᕆᔭᐅᓪᓗᓂ. ᓂᕿᖕᒋᓪᓕ ᐊᕐᕌᒍᓕᒫᖅ ᓂᕆᔭᐅᕙᒃᑐᑦ, ᑭᓯᐊᓂ ᒪᒪᕐᓂᖅᐹᙳᔪᑦ ᐅᐱᕐᖓᒃᓵᒃᑯᑦ ᒫᓕᕌᖓᑦ.

The ringed seal is the smallest seal in the Arctic. When ringed seals are born, they are bright white, but they soon turn silver. Adult ringed seals are dark gray with light gray ring marks on their backs. Baby ringed seals stay with their mother for the first two months of life, but then take care of themselves. In winter, ringed seals live under the sea ice. They dig holes through the ice so they can breathe. Sometimes they rest on the ice in small caves, which they carve into snowdrifts. But they are always ready to slip into the water if they sense danger. The ringed seal is a very important part of Inuit life. The skins of ringed seals are used to make pants, mittens, boots, and kayaks, and ringed seal fat is used for the *qulliq*, a traditional lamp. The meat is eaten all year round, but tastes best when the seal is shedding its fur in early spring.

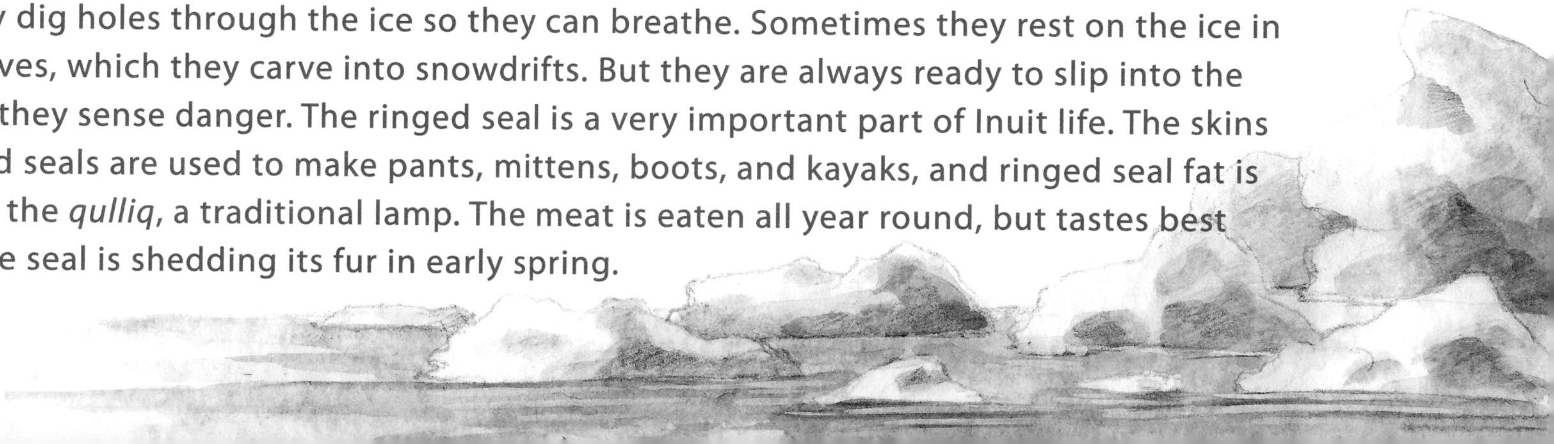

ᖃᐃᕿᓕᒃ | Harp Seal

ᖃᐃᕿᓖᑦ ᖃᑦᑐᓈᑎᑐᑦ ᑎᑕᐅᑎᑐᑦ ᐊᑎᖃᖅᑎᑕᐅᕗᑦ ᒥᖅᑯᐊᓂ ᑕᖅᓴᖏᑦ ᐱᑦᑐᒋᑦ. ᐃᒪᕐᒥᐅᑕᑎᑐᑦ ᐊᓯᒥᒃᑎᑐᑦ ᐱᕋᙱᑦᑐᑦ ᐊᒥᓱᐊᓘᑦᑐᑎᒃ ᑲᑎᙵᑦᑐᑎᒃ ᐱᕋᒃᑐᑦ. ᐊᐅᔭᒃᑯᑦ ᓄᓇᕗᑦ ᐃᓚᖓᓃᓯᑦ ᐊᒻᒪᓗ ᐊᑯᑭᑦᑐᑦ ᐃᒪᖓᓃᓯᑦ. ᐅᑭᐊᒃᓵᒃᑯᑦ ᑕᐅᓄᙵᖅᐸᒃᑐᑦ ᓂᐅᕋᓐ ᓛᓐ ᐃᒪᖓᓄᑦ ᐊᒻᒪ ᑕᒫᓂ ᓵᖓᓂ ᓴᐃᓐ ᓗᐊᕆᓐᔅ. ᓯᑯᑦ ᖄᖓᓃᓯᑦ ᐊᐅᔭᒃᑯᑦ ᓂᒡᓚᓱᒃᑐᒎᖓᐅᓚᐅᙱᓐᓂᕐᒥᖕᓂ. ᐃᒪᕐᒥᐅᑕᓚᒫᑎᑐᑦ ᐃᒪᐅᙱᑦᑐᒥ ᐊᔪᖅᑐᑦ ᖃᓄᐃᓕᐅᕆᓱᒃᑐᑎᒃ ᑭᓯᐊᓂ ᐃᒫᓂ ᐊᔪᙱᑦᑐᐊᓗᐃᑦ. ᐊᑯᓂᐅᓂᖃᖅᑐᒥᒃ 15 ᒥᓂᒥᒃ ᐃᒫᓂ ᐊᖅᑲᐅᒪᔪᓐᓇᖅᑐᑦ. ᑭᓱᑐᐃᓐᓇᓂᒃ ᓂᕆᔪᓐᓇᖅᑐᑦ ᖃᐃᕿᓖᑦ, ᐆᒐᕐᓂᒡᓗ, ᕿᙳᒃᐸᖕᓂᒃᓗ ᓂᕆᕙᖕᒥᔪᑦ.

The harp seal is named for the harp-shaped black bands on its body. Unlike other seals, harp seals live in large groups. In the summer, they live in northeastern Nunavut and western Greenland. In the fall, they migrate south to Newfoundland and the Gulf of St. Lawrence. There, they live on pack ice until they travel north again in the summer. Like all seals, harp seals are clumsy on ice, but are excellent swimmers. They can stay under water for up to fifteen minutes. Harp seals eat just about anything they can catch, including codfish and shrimp.

ᐊᐃᕕᖅ | Walrus

ᓇᑦᑏᑦ ᐃᓚᖁᑎᖏᑦ ᐊᐃᕖᑦ ᐊᖑᑎᖅᐸᐅᔪᖓᑦ ᔭᓕᕆᐊᒡᒥ. ᑯᔨᑎᒌᔫᔪᕐᑦ ᑕᑭᔪᐊᓗᖕᓂᒃ ᐊᒥᐊᒡᑯᑦ ᑐᒑᑦᑯᒡᑖᖏᑦᑯᑎᒃ ᐊᒡᒪ ᐊᖅᐹᓴᖅᒥᑕᔨᖓᑦᑯᑎᒃ ᐅᖙᒃᒃᔫᖏᑦ ᔭᒃᖅᑕᕐᖁᑦ ᔮᓗᑎᒃᖓᑦ. ᑕᑯᐹᔪᖓᑦᑏᑦ ᑮᔨᒃᔫᖏᑦ ᖁᑉᖅᒡᖓᑦ, ᑮᔨᐊᓂ ᐃᓪᒃᔫᖓᑦ ᐊᒡᐹᕐᔨᖅᔫᐸᐅᖁᓐᑦ. ᐊᒡᐃᑦ ᐊᔪᑎᖓᑦ ᐊᐃᖅᑦ ᑎᒥᒃᖁᔨᖅᐊᔪᖓᖅᖁᑦᖁᒃᑏᑦ ᐊᒡᐃᑦ ᐊᖅᖓᔪᖅᒡᒥ ᑕᐃᔪᐸᖅᔫᖓᖁᑦ. ᐊᐃᕖᑦ ᐊᒡᔮᒡᔮᒡᖅᔫᔪᕐᑦ ᓂᓕᔪᔫᕐᑦ, ᑮᔨᐊᓐᑦᑖᖅ ᐊᔪᑎᖓᖅ ᐴᒡᖓᖓᑦ ᓂᓕᖅᖁᒡᑖᖁᒃᑏᑦ ᓇᑦᑎᒡᖁᑉ ᑎᒃᒡᐊᒡᖁᑉ ᐊᒡᒪᑉ ᖁᖓᔪᖅᖁᑉᖓᑦ. ᐊᐃᕖᑦ ᐊᖅᖓᖅᐅᒡᒥᒃᔫᔪᕐᑦ ᑕᑯᖅᖓ ᐃᖅᖅᐊᒡᔫᓐᑦ ᐅᒃᐁᔫᒡᖁᑦ ᒡᔨᔨᔫᒡᖁᒃ ᓂᖅᖅᒃᒃᔨᒃᐅᔫᒡᖓᖁᑦ. ᑕᐃᒃᖓ ᐳᐁᖅᔫᖁᑦ ᐊᖅᖅᖁᖓᖅᖅᐸᔫᒡᖁᑦ ᐊᖁᖅᐊᒡᔨ ᓂᖅᐁᒃᔫᑦ ᑕᐃᒃᖓ. ᐃᖅᖅᖁᑦ ᔮᓕᒡᒥᑉ ᐊᔮᖅᑕᐅᖅᐊᒡᐅᖅᔫᒡᑦ ᖓᒡᑯᔨᐊᔪᖅᔫᖁᑦ ᔮᖅᒃᖁᐊᔨᖁᖅᖁᑉᔨ ᐊᒡᒪᔫᖅᑕᐅᖅ ᐅᖁᖅᐊᔨᖅᔫᒡᖁᑦ. ᐊᒡᒪᖅᖁᑖᖅ ᓴᖁᔫᐊᒡᖁᐊᖁᐊᔨᔪᔫᖅᖅᖓᑦᑯᑕᐅᖅᔫᖁᑦ. ᐊᒡᒪ ᖁᖅᔫᖅᒃ ᖅᒡᔨᔫᒡᖁᒡᑦ ᐁᔮᖁᖅᖓᖅᖅᐁᒡᖁᑦ ᐊᒡᒪ ᐊᔨᒃᒡᖁᖅᖓ ᓂᖅᖅᔨᔨᖅᐁᒡᒃᖓ.

The walrus is the largest species of seal in the Arctic. Walruses have very long canine teeth, which form their unique tusks, and short, thick whiskers on their snouts. Their skin appears brown when they are on land, but underwater the walrus's skin is a much lighter pinkish colour. Male walruses are called bulls and females are called cows. Walruses eat mostly clams, but they will also feed on seals, birds, and beluga whales. Walruses dive beneath the ice for five to ten minutes at a time searching for food. They will dive again and again for several hours before they have found enough food to satisfy their appetites. Walrus tusks are used by Inuit to create harpoon heads and harpoon shafts. These tusks can also be carved into beautiful sculptures. Walrus skin can be used the runners on *qamutiik*, sleds, and every part of the walrus can be eaten.

25

ᖅᐸᓗᒐᖅ (ᐊᑦᑕᕐᔪᐊᖅ) | Narwhal

ᖅᐸᓗᒐᐃᑦ ᐊᖕᕈᐊᕐᑎᓈᔪ ᒥᕿᐊᕐᑎᓈᔪ ᑕᐃᒪᑦᑐᑦ. ᐊᖕᐅᑎᑦ ᑐᒃᖄᖅᑐᑦ ᖅᐱᔪᓕᖅᖅᑐᓂᒃ ᖃᓂᖕᒪᑕ ᖅᑯᔾᒍᑦ ᐱᑕᖅᐸᓕᐊᕐᒃᑐᑦ. ᑕᑭᓂᖃᓕᖕ ᐆᑐᖄᐅᑦ ᐱᖕᒪᕐᐱᐊᖅᕐᓱᒍ. ᐃᑦᖕᓂᒃᑕᑦ ᒪᕐᖓᓂᒃ ᑐᒃᖄᑲᑦᐱᖁᔪᑦ ᑐᓂᑦᑲᑦᑕᕐᓂᒃ ᓇᐃᖕᓂᖅᒥᖕ. ᑌᐊᑕ ᐃᐊᒃᒥᑕᑦᑕᓂᑦ ᑕᐸᕐᓂᒃᐅᔾᔫᒃᐱᐊᖅᖅᓪᖅᑦ ᐊᖅᑲᐅᒪᔾᔪᒃᑦ. ᑕᐸᕐᓂᒃᐅᔾᔪᓂᒃ ᓂᕐᖅᑐᔾᔪᖕᒪᑦᑕ ᐃᖅᓄᖕᓂᑦᓄᔭ,ᑭᔾᒃᐸᖕᓂᑦᓄᔭ, ᐊᒻᒪ ᐊᔾᖕᓂᒃ. ᖅᐸᓗᒐᐃᑦ ᐊᒪᔾᒃ ᐃᖕᓂᖅᕐᑐᓂᒃ ᑲᑎᒪᔪᒃ ᑕᒥᓇ 15-ᓕᑐ 20-ᓄ ᑕᐃᒪᓄᐊ ᐆᒃᖕᑎᓕᑐᓂᒃ ᐱᔾᒃ ᑭᔭᐊᓂ ᐃᐊᖕᓂᒃ ᑲᑎᒪᔾᒃ ᐊᒥᔾᒪᒃᑕᐊᓴᔾᒃᑦ. ᑕᑭᑐᐊ ᐱᐊᔾᒃᑕᕐᔾᒃ ᑐᒃᔾᒃᕐᔭᖁᒃ ᐊᒻᒪᓗ ᒪᒃᑕᕐᔾᖁᒃ. ᐃᐆᖕᓂᒃ ᒪᒃᑕᒃᓇ ᓂᕐᔾᐅᔾᖅ. ᑎᒥᒃᑦ ᐱᐊᕈᓂᒃ ᐱᖅᕐᓕᑲ ᓂᕐᔾᐅᔾᖁᖕᒃ. ᐊᖕᕖᓈᔾᖕᑦ ᐅᖅᔾᒃᑯᔾᒃ ᑕᒃᑕᐊ ᑐᒃᓂᑦ ᐱᔾᓴᕐᖕᓂᖕᓂᖕᖅᓘᖅᑕᒃᒍᖅ ᖃᑕᑐᖅᑕᓂᑦ ᑕᐸᕈᓂ ᐃᑎᕐᔾᒃᑯᔾᖕᒃᒃ.

Narwhals are medium-sized whales. Male narwhals have a spiraled tusk that grows from their upper left jaw. The tusk grows up to three metres long. Sometimes, a second tusk grows from the right side of the jaw. Occasionally, female narwhals also have tusks, but their tusks are much smaller. Narwhals can swim deeper than any other marine mammal. They dive down to catch fish, shrimp, and squid. Narwhals live in groups of about fifteen to twenty individuals, but sometimes they gather in the thousands. Narwhals are hunted for their ivory tusks and *muktuk*, their outer layer of skin and fat. Narwhal skin is an important food source for Inuit. It is high in vitamin C and other nutrients. Hunters say that narwhals are more difficult to catch than beluga whales because narwhals like to stay in deeper waters.

ᓇᓄᖅ | Polar Bear

ᓇᓄᐃᑦ ᐊᖏᓂᖅᐸᐅᔪᑦ ᓯᒃᓯᐊᕈᒥ. ᐊᖑᑕᐅᔪᖕᓂ ᓇᓄᖅ ᓇᓴᐸᐅᑎᑐᑦ ᒥᑦᑕᑐᑦ ᐅᕐᖢᓛᖕᓂᖃᖅᐸᒃᑐᖅ. ᓇᓄᐃᑦ ᐊᖖᒐᓇᖅᑲᔪᐃᑦ. ᓯᒃᑲᓱᑎᓗ ᓴᖖᒐᕙᔾᓱᑎᓗ. ᐊᒻᒪ ᐃᒪᒧᑦ ᐊᖏᕐᖃᑦᔪᑐᑎᒃ. ᐊᒻᒪᓗ ᐱᖅᑐᖅᑎᒍᑦ ᒪᖁᕐᒐᔾᐅᕐᒃ ᖁᕐᖕᑦᒃ ᐃᐱᒃᑐᐊᔾᖓᑕ. ᓂᑎᓂᐊᖅᑕᒥᒃ ᐃᒪᓂᒃ ᐊᒍᖦᐊᒃᑐᑦ ᑭᒍᑎᖓᑦᓗ ᐃᒃᒥᖓᑦᓗ ᓴᖖᒐᕙᔾᓗᑕ. ᓇᐃᑕᓐᑎᐊᖅᑐᐊᔾᐱᑕ – ᓇᐃᓕᖑᖅᑐᑦ ᓇᑎᐱᕝ ᐊᓱᖏᕐᖕᓂᖅ ᑭᖓᑦᒧᕆᒃ ᐅᖕᓴᔮᖕᓂᖅᖃᑐᒦᒃ. ᓂᖕᑭᓂᖅᐸᓇᖁᕝᖃᐊᕐᔭ ᐊᑕᓐᐱᕝ ᐅᖅᔮᕐᕝ ᐊᒻᒪ ᐊᔨᕐᕝ ᐃᒪᖅᒦᑕᒃᓂᕐᖕ. ᓂᐱᔭᖏᖅᒦᖕᕝ ᓴᔨᓕᖅᕝᖃᐸᑐᑐᑦ ᐃᒪᓇᐊᖅᖢᑎᒃ ᐊᒻᒪ ᐊᔭᓐᑐᒃ ᓴᔨᓕᖅᕝᖃᖅᑐᑎᒃ. ᐊᖅᓴᓐᔾᖖᔮᕐᑐᑕᕐ ᐱᓪᐱᒃ, ᐃᔾᖅᔾᒪᐅᓇᕐᔾᑐᑎᒃ ᐅᑭᐅᖃᑐᒃ. ᐃᓚᖖᓂᒃ ᐊᐱᓐᑎᖕᓂ (ᑎᔾᒦᖕᓂ) ᐃᔾᖅᔾᒪᐃᑦ ᓯᑕᕆᓐᑦᒦᖢᔾ, ᑭᔭᓇᒃ ᐅᑭᐅᑲᐃᖅ ᓯᓂᔾᖖᔮᕐᑐᑦ.

The polar bear is the largest bear in the world. An adult polar bear may weigh as much as a small car! Polar bears are skilled hunters. They are fast and strong. They are excellent swimmers and they can climb icebergs with their sharp claws. They drag prey out of the water with their powerful paws and jaw. Polar bears also have good noses—they can smell a seal breathing hole from up to a kilometre away. Their main diet is the fat from seals and other ocean animals. After they eat, polar bears clean themselves by swimming, or by rubbing their heads in snow. Unlike black bears and grizzly bears, polar bears do not hibernate. Sometimes they rest in dens to escape stormy weather, but they do not sleep through the winter.

ᐲᒥ ᖃᐃᕈᖅ
Romi Caron

ᓕᐊ ᐅᑕᒃ
Leah Otak

ᓗᐃᔅ ᕝᓚᓲᐊᕐᑎ
Louise Flaherty

ᔅᑎᐊᕙᓂ ᒪᒃᑖᓄᓪᑦ
Stephanie McDonald

ᑐᓂᓯᔨᑦ | Contributors

ᐋᓇ ᓯᒡᓗᖅ
Anna Ziegler

ᓴᐃᒪᓐ ᐊᕙ
Simon Awa

ᓯᒡᓗᒃ ᐊᖅᑭᐊᒍᖅ
Seeglook Akeeagok